EVERYTHING I LEARNED
ABOUT PEOPLE,
I LEARNED FROM
A ROUND OF GOLF

EVERYTHING I LEARNED ABOUT PEOPLE, I LEARNED FROM A ROUND OF GOLF

JOHN ANDRISANI

ALPHA
A Pearson Education Company

Copyright © 2002 by John Andrisani

All rights reserved. No part of this book shall be reproduced, stored in a retrieval system, or transmitted by any means, electronic, mechanical, photocopying, recording, or otherwise, without written permission from the publisher. No patent liability is assumed with respect to the use of the information contained herein. Although every precaution has been taken in the preparation of this book, the publisher and author assume no responsibility for errors or omissions. Neither is any liability assumed for damages resulting from the use of information contained herein. For information, address Alpha Books, 201 West 103rd Street, Indianapolis, IN 46290.

International Standard Book Number: 0-02-864342-9

Library of Congress Catalog Card Number: 2002101643

04   03   02   8   7   6   5   4   3   2   1

Interpretation of the printing code: The rightmost number of the first series of numbers is the year of the book's printing; the rightmost number of the second series of numbers is the number of the book's printing. For example, a printing code of 02-1 shows that the first printing occurred in 2002.

Printed in the United States of America

Note: This publication contains the opinions and ideas of its author. It is intended to provide helpful and informative material on the subject matter covered. It is sold with the understanding that the author and publisher are not engaged in rendering professional services in the book. If the reader requires personal assistance or advice, a competent professional should be consulted.

The author and publisher specifically disclaim any responsibility for any liability, loss, or risk, personal or otherwise, which is incurred as a consequence, directly or indirectly, of the use and application of any of the contents of this book.

Trademarks

All terms mentioned in this book that are known to be or are suspected of being trademarks or service marks have been appropriately capitalized. Alpha Books and Pearson Education, Inc., cannot attest to the accuracy of this information. Use of a term in this book should not be regarded as affecting the validity of any trademark or service mark.

For marketing and publicity, please call: 317-581-3722

The publisher offers discounts on this book when ordered in quantity for bulk purchases and special sales.

For sales within the United States, please contact: Corporate and Government Sales, 1-800-382-3419 or corpsales@pearsontechgroup.com

Outside the United States, please contact: International Sales, 317-581-3793 or international@pearsontechgroup.com

I dedicate this book to the go-getter golfers in this world who know that good scoring is not just about writing numbers down on a card and adding them up at the end of the day. Being able to read people and depend on intelligent tactics to make a positive on-course connection—a score—is the secret to developing a solid business association, love relationship, or lasting friendship.

Contents

Foreword

When John Andrisani, a friend and golf partner, told me he was writing *Everything I Learned About People, I Learned from a Round of Golf*, I was excited and extremely anxious to read the final draft copy of the manuscript that had been delivered to me prior to publication.

John taught golf earlier in his life at various country clubs, which is one reason he is such a good people person and personality reader. After regaining his amateur status, he also spent time playing with top golf teachers and tour pros while senior editor of instruction at *GOLF Magazine*. During his long stint at *GOLF* from 1982 to 1998, and today, too, he does a lot of entertaining on the golf course and at the club. It's obvious from reading the book you now hold in your hands that all this experience has enabled him to build a strong database of human characteristics—good, bad, and ugly personality traits—and thus made it easier for him to read people.

What makes this book fun to read is that you recognize mannerisms of golfers you play with, but now you learn how to interpret the truth behind their words and body language so that you can be a step ahead of the game going on within the game. Not until reading John's new book did I realize to what degree you could take the analysis process and learn so much about a person before, during, and after a game of golf. Trust me, Sigmund Freud would be proud of this practical guide to learning what you really need to know about your opponents, clients, and friends.

I'm the author of the best-selling book *Power Networking*, the CEO of Coach U (the largest training company in the world), and a golfer to boot. So I've known for a long time that the golf course is an excellent meeting place. In fact, for many years it's been a secondary office of mine—as it has been for other successful businessmen and businesswomen golfers, such as real estate genius Donald Trump, sports management guru Mark McCormack, actor Jack Nicholson, actress Cheryl Ladd, and PGA Tour pro and entrepreneur Greg Norman.

The strongest golf course "base" used by savvy golfers to observe clients and do coaching has been the 19th hole. I agree with John that it's better to depend on multiple bases—to look, listen, and learn before the round and during the round, too, working really hard to connect with a person while riding in the golf cart together.

With the publication of *Everything I Learned About People, I Learned from a Round of Golf*, John is sure to strike a chord with golfers looking for new ways to make a business or social connection. As a trained personal coach, I thought I was an expert at assessing people until I read this book.

This book educates people of varying income levels and positions on the value of using golf in business. It also includes an in-depth analysis of conducting customer golf, from the host's and guest's perspectives. John explains the art of conducting business on the golf course, both intelligently and at a highly sophisticated level; his long experience has taught him how to work all the right angles—directly, indirectly, and honestly.

One of John's objectives as a golf insider was to peel away, for the very first time, the confusion and intimidation behind using golf as a successful business tool. Make no mistake; he

x

succeeds, explaining the ins and outs of how to win the high-stakes game of customer golf.

There is no competition for *Everything I Learned About People, I Learned from a Round of Golf,* a book that offers great insights into learning how to mingle with people on the course, how to act, and how to react. This authoritative how-to guide reveals the do's and don'ts of customer golf and is complete with tips on how the game *really* works among high-echelon businessmen. After you read it, you can't help but understand the rules for playing the people game in your new outdoor office where it is anything but business as usual.

There is no question that if you are a CEO of a big corporation or even a small business owner, you have purchased the right book—for you and your employees. Many companies sponsor one-day golf outings at courses around the country—with the goal being to have employees play with potential clients and get them into business relationships. Fun, intelligent interchanges over a period of a few hours on the course, good conversation about life and business over drinks at the 19th hole, exchanging business cards, and making a date for future golf games should be the order of the day. But often, these golf goals fail to come to fruition. The reason is that many golfers don't know the first thing about playing business golf and reading people. This book is the ultimate training tool because it will enable employees to learn how to work the room on the course, build contacts, and create added revenue through new sales.

Everything I Learned About People, I Learned from a Round of Golf also goes far beyond the realm of applying what you learn about reading people and understanding them to make deals or climb the business ladder. What really sets this book apart is that you can apply the knowledge you gain to help you find good friends, or maybe even a lifetime mate, through golf. This book is, in fact, a vital weapon to take with you to the course so that you are armed and ready to strengthen existing personal relationships or deal and defeat sharks of one kind or another, male or female.

The golf course has become the ideal place to network for just about everyone. And if you are ambitious and follow John's suggestions and countermeasures, you are very likely to succeed—no matter who you are. If you are a high school student, you can meet someone on the course who can help you get into a leading university or start you in a stockbroker training program after you graduate. If you are a roofer who works only on homes, you can meet someone who can get you into more lucrative commercial work. If you are a young lawyer, you can meet a veteran attorney who might recruit you into his or her firm or, at least, steer you to some good contacts. If you're a nurse, you can meet a doctor on the course who can help you secure a job at a top hospital. The list goes on.

On the links, if you play your cards right, it's often a win-win situation. In *Everything I Learned About People, I Learned from a Round of Golf*, John certainly provides you with what it takes to do your part.

Sandy Vilas
CEO of Coach U
Author of *Power Networking*

Introduction

"People reading is a matter of opening up your senses to what is really going on and converting this insight into tangible evidence that you can use to your advantage."

—Mark McCormack, from his best-selling book, *What They Don't Teach You at Harvard Business School*

Everything I Learned About People, I Learned from a Round of Golf is not like any book you are accustomed to seeing in the golf section at your local bookstore; it is neither instructional, biographical, nor historical in nature. Rather, it is a guidebook for learning how to analyze people you play golf with and to determine their true personalities—everybody from a new friend to a potential business client—by watching his or her actions before, during, and after the game. For example, your seemingly good-mannered client suddenly throws a club after hitting a bad shot, which is a sign that he is unpredictable in business situations. The person you've recently started dating constantly makes excuses for his or her poor play, showing that he or she is insecure and easily swayed. Some people will lie about their handicap, which shows that they cannot be trusted. And what can you learn at the 19th hole? Between how your playing partners order, what they order, and how they behave at the table in the club, you can make a round of golf more valuable than a lunch at "21."

Golfing with business associates, colleagues, friends, clients, and partners can be an important way to network, gain information, close deals, and spend time with people. Based on my long experience in the golf world and years of observing players, I will provide you with people-reading secrets that will enable you to get the inside track on your golf guests and understand what their actions say about them. I'll teach you how to evaluate others from the moment you pick up the telephone to invite them out to play golf. And I'll tell you how to evaluate men and women as you play golf with them and spend time together after the round.

There's a big difference between going out with someone and moving in with him or her or getting married. The same is true about going into business with a friend who you have always respected for his or her good points and been able to forgive the bad points such as always being late. In business, you find that letting this same friend slide and get away with things is a shortcut to financial disaster. This one-of-a-kind book provides you with a crash course in learning about people skills, specifically how to read a client, convert a deal, and save a deal. It also teaches you how to identify such things as the difference between winners and losers so that you make the right decisions in your personal life and enjoy your time on earth with someone who's good for you.

These days, especially, with more and more people having to tighten their purse strings, you cannot afford to make a mistake. The emotional trauma and financial stress of a relationship gone sour or a business venture going south can be very hard to deal with. The tactics I teach you in this book will enable you to do such a good job of reading people that you will be less likely to make a mistake in judgment. At the end of the day, I guarantee you will know the difference between who's a good bet and who's a bad bet. The reason I say this is because in *Everything I Learned About People, I Learned from a Round of Golf*, I teach you to use common sense and proceed with caution when choosing whom you get involved with. I also convince you to adopt a philosophy that enables you to focus on identifying personality blocks and eliminating them so that a compromise is possible.

If you have ever played poker with cards or liar's poker with dollar bills, you know how much fun it can be, learning about how people think by the calls they make, the *tells* they reveal through their physical actions (namely eye movement and the sound of their voice). Believe me, the intrigue of playing a cat-and-mouse game on the golf course can be even more amusing—provided you have what it takes to figure out a person's true colors and use tactics and countermeasures that enable you to maneuver like a general and win battles.

Everything I Learned About People, I Learned from a Round of Golf teaches you how to make the right moves so that you can put your best foot forward—before the golf game, during the golf game, and after the golf game. But it is by no means an etiquette book. I say this because the "acting" tips contained within it go far beyond the basics. By following my strategies and learning how to look for good points in people, you discover the secrets to better assessing a client's value or a friend's reliability.

Because you are reading this book, you are probably very serious about improving your financial status by virtue of making good business decisions involving others. This is a good sign because when it comes to business, George Bernard Shaw was right when he said, "It is not money that is the root of all evil, but the lack of money that is the root of all evil." This book is sure to help you succeed in business, but not without trying. You must read my secrets to understanding people, and then apply the most strategic countermeasures I teach you.

If you are reading this book to improve your personal life through golf, that's okay, too. When it comes to relationships outside of business, I say that it is not love but the lack of love that is the root of all evil. Let the golf course be your new dating venue after you finish this book because it is there that you will learn so much about a potential significant other or a person you see as possibly becoming a new friend. In just one round, I promise that you will know whether you are right or wrong about someone.

By purchasing this book, you move a step closer to attaining success through golf that millions of others are cheating themselves out of. Individuals from all walks of life are playing golf, but because of a lack of knowledge, many are failing to meet someone who can help them grow financially or personally. This is the first guidebook for teaching you course-smart skills that you can apply to your life so that you no longer have to wait for fate to control your future. I am giving you the tools for finding success on the golf course. Now, go for it!

To help you "score" on the course, this book teaches you the signs to watch for in others and directs you on the right path. For example, getting ready the evening before for your big day, your instructions include setting your alarm, cleaning and counting your clubs, preparing the right clothes, and mentally mapping out your objectives. Countermeasures such as these help you make the best impression by arriving at the club on time and dressing the part, and they can give you the best chance of being a hit on the course and attaining your objectives. If your golf guest fails to do the right things, such as to be prompt, this gives you an advantage.

Everything I Learned About People, I Learned from a Round of Golf not only provides you valuable information about reading people, it also helps you make a plan and put into practice what you've learned. I show you how to track a person's good and bad points. What's more, to be sure you correctly read your playing partner, extra pages have been provided at the back of the book. Use these to record observations, personal details, preferences such as your guest's favorite wine, perfume, cigars, golf clubs, and so on. That way, you will get in the habit of looking and learning on the links.

Acknowledgments

I thank my agent Scott Waxman for bringing my idea for reading people and making connections on the golf course to Renee Wilmeth at Alpha Books. She has helped take my idea and turn it into a practical guide for learning what you really need to know about making new male and female friends and exciting business associations through golf. Not only was her title *Everything I Learned About People, I Learned from a Round of Golf* right on the mark, but she was also a tremendous help to me in the creative process.

I'm grateful to Patrick O'Shea, a neighbor of mine growing up on Long Island, New York, for introducing me to golf; my mother, a people person par excellence, for teaching me sensitivity through her advice and poetry; and my father for passing on athletic genes. These three people, the golf pros I grew up around as a boy, and the members of Bellport Country Club who I caddied for and played with, helped me make the connection between people skills and golf skills.

Someone who understands where I'm coming from and has applied his people skills to making "scores" on the golf course is Sandy Vilas, who was so kind to write the foreword to this book. Vilas is the author of the best-selling book *Power Networking* and the CEO of Coach U, a company that offers invaluable guidance and advice to everyday people and top-echelon individuals from the world of business and finance.

As to the expert production of this book, I thank the team of editors, artists, and other in-house pros at Alpha Books, a division of Pearson Education, Inc.

Before the Golf Game

Getting to Know Your

Playing Partner Should Be

Your Chief Priority

The expression "life is what you make of it" certainly applies to the first part of this book. Setting up a game of golf requires good planning and some risk taking. To succeed on the country-club front, you must take time to conduct research and learn about a golfer who invites you to play, and you must be confident and prepared to pick up the telephone and ask someone you want to get to know better to play. In this part, I help you lay the groundwork for making your golf experience a big success by teaching you how to read a person even before the two of you play the golf course.

The preround process requires patience and perseverance. At this stage, you must listen more than talk. Just go back in time and recall the early phone call you made to someone you found attractive in high school, and you'll know what I mean. Before you made "the call," you probably made inquiries about the person and thought hard about where you would go on a date. What's more, when you finally mustered up the courage to pick up the telephone and call, you found yourself stopping midway through the number and hanging up the receiver. Only after becoming confident or convincing yourself that you had nothing to lose did you dial the number. Once on the phone, you got the words out, suggesting a date and listening to your heart pound as you waited for an answer. After the date was set, you started to worry about what to wear in order to make the best impression. Likely, too, you worried yourself to death about how the date would go. Then, on the night of the date, while driving to the movies or some such destination, there was the inevitable small talk and sweaty palms to deal with. While at the movies, you waited for that special moment, a signal. You watched body language and listened carefully to every word until you felt the timing was right. At that point, you embraced. You had broken through the barrier and could now open up and be yourself.

The golf-date experience is very similar. On your way to establishing, say, a lasting and valuable business association or social relationship, you will experience a variety of emotions and need to break through internal and external barriers. In achieving your goals, you must show strength by taking the initiative. More important, though, is that you must be strong enough to be understanding of the other person's needs, particularly if that new golf friend of yours is someone you have a romantic interest in.

When dealing with people, it's true that the devil you know is better than the devil you don't know. I say this not to suggest that humans are deceitful. We all sometimes put on different masks or faces when we first meet someone. The shortcut to being successful—in this case, before the golf game—is to determine the other person's true character. This unveiling technique requires you to ask the right questions at the right time. Additionally, it requires you to listen intently to the other person's answers, all the time carefully observing his or her physical movements. It's this analytical procedure that will enable you to predict how the other person will respond on the course and to take the proper countermeasures to win him or her over.

Actual proven tactics for coming out on top will be discussed in Part 2, "During the Golf Game." For now, it's critical that you establish a strong foundation and keep one Chinese proverb in mind: "Every journey starts with one small step."

Many times in my own life, it's been the work I did before the round that made the difference. In fact, when I know I'll be playing with an editor, publisher, golf teacher, or tour pro, I still take a moment to prepare. Then I can take advantage of an opening in a conversation by planting the seed for writing a magazine article or book. To succeed in business or in personal relationships through golf, you must do your homework, tactfully arrange the game, make follow-up phone calls to secure the time and meeting place, prepare properly the evening before, make a good first impression when arriving at the course, be a good host, be a well-mannered guest, know the secrets for getting the other person to open up during preround practice, be cautious about betting too much, and know the right jokes to tell during the downtime prior to teeing off.

You can see already that the work involved before the game even begins is vital and must be well thought out. In short, you cannot wing it.

Doing Your Homework

In today's supercompetitive environment, you must be extra careful when getting involved in personal or business relationships. Face it, there's a lot at stake, and nobody likes wasting valuable time making the wrong strategic moves. Mistakes can lead you to opportunists and crooks rather than to solid friendships, beneficial business associates, and financial success. So before going on a golf date with someone new, take a cautionary measure of checking out your guest in advance—taking advantage of the insights of others as well as doing solid research on your own.

Playing with a friend or an acquaintance is one thing, but playing with Mr. or Ms. X whom you've never met before is another. Go into the research mode so that you get an early read on the "mystery person." Telephone friends, fax business associates, write a short note with questions, and send out a few e-mails to find out anything you can about the person you are going to be playing with. It does not matter whether he or she invited you or you did the inviting. Discreetly find out what you can about the person's personality traits and golf skills so that you can form a visual picture and start thinking early of measures that will enable you to make the best impression. Be careful, however, not to seem overanxious. Otherwise, you could blow your chance of making a solid business or social connection.

When asking about a person's golf handicap, try to determine whether he or she plays to it. Your key objective is to gain enough inside information to be forewarned about a hustler who scores well below his or her official handicap or a hacker who scores well above his or her handicap.

If the reason you're setting up the golf game is business-oriented, do a little extra sleuthing to find out the person's reputation. Although you'll be using the game to make your own judgements, it is sometimes helpful to know in advance if he or she is known as a person who sticks to his or her word or is open-minded enough to listen to your suggestions for joint growth.

In gathering your insights about your new playing partner from such sources as your friends or their business associates, follow the Godfather's advice: "Use creditable people." You want people who can tell the difference between someone being shy and being a snob, for example. Opinions that come from people who aren't savvy can cause you to prejudge an individual and make a serious mistake. Always proceed with caution, too, when doing any pregame investigative work so that you don't come off as an insecure snoop. Listen carefully to the opinions of others, while at the same time taking everything with a grain of salt. Failing to take this approach can lead you to be overly encouraged or discouraged.

Independent, but Incomplete Research

If the person you are scheduled to play with is a star in his or her industry and you are looking to make a favorable impression on the golf course, read up on the person in books, magazines, and on the Internet prior to your game. This prep work will enable you to ask intelligent questions when you meet. By the same token, if you conduct incomplete research and don't dig deep enough, you will get stuck as I once did, putting yourself on the defense.

When I scheduled a game with a famous movie actor a few years ago at the Garden City Golf Club on Long Island, I called one of his best friends, a restaurant owner and writer of cookbooks. In preparing for my golf date, I asked this friend a lot of questions. More important, however, I read numerous articles and made sure that there was not one movie the actor had made that I hadn't seen or at least heard about. The reason I worked so hard was that I was hoping to get the job of ghost-writing his autobiography.

On the morning of the match, the actor's limousine picked me up at my hotel, and then drove me to where the actor and his friend were staying.

I was in the back seat of the limousine with Mr. Big-Time Movie Star, thinking that he was going to talk golf or movies. Instead, he pulled out *The Wall Street Journal* and started discussing stocks. A half hour later, he had the limousine driver stop the car, open the trunk, and put in a rap music CD he wanted to hear. I managed to hold up my end of the stock conversation. However, when it came to him asking me about what rap groups I liked, I was at a complete loss.

Had I known this guy was into rap, I would have gotten familiar with the music beforehand so that I could hold my own in conversation. Incomplete research hurt me. I felt I made a poor first impression, and during the round, the actor was fairly quiet, too. It was clear that he only felt comfortable talking to his friend. After the round, he seemed to loosen up, but the slow start hurt any chance of building a lasting rapport.

Another aspect of this situation was how the dynamic was changed when he was playing with his friend, who played closer to his level. If I'd wanted to try to develop a relationship from which I might have launched a business idea, I might have been better off having his friend arrange a game for just me and the actor. A one-on-one situation is always more conducive to reading people and to making a personal or business connection. I could also have made sure that we had as much opportunity to talk as possible. For example, I could have arranged for golf carts rather than caddies so that I could have ridden with the actor and been positioned to converse freely with him. I learned first hand that if I'd planned ahead better, the situation might have had a different outcome.

As usual, this is easy to say in hindsight. The fact is that sometimes you can do all the research in the world and still fail to make a connection. At least I gave it the old college try.

Sooner or later, you will run into someone who talks a good game ("I used to be scratch"), drives the right cars, wears an expensive watch, lives in an upscale neighborhood, belongs to a high-priced club, and says he or she can make you rich. The thing is, after several meetings, you still have not figured out exactly what this person does for a living. The so-called "investment banker" knows every maitre d' in town and seems to be into everything from stocks to bonds to wines to diamonds. Now you are invited to play golf. What do you do after your research turns up nothing?

Granted, the person could be for real. Nevertheless, if you are smart, you will check the person out *before* your scheduled game to see if he or she is genuine.

Invite him or her out to the driving range—"Hey, what do you say we go hit some balls at the range and stop for a drink afterward?" If the person says no or agrees but then cancels, it could be a sign that he or she is evasive. Should the person show up, hit the ball badly, and start making excuses, chances are he or she might not be who you think. If the person hits poorly and asks for pointers, you're probably dealing with someone more sincere.

I don't think you should go to the extreme of running a pregame background check on a suspect person. Besides, the golf course is where you will do your best reading. Having said that, you must be careful. A couple of years ago, two notorious con artists were bilking people out of millions: One ran around the Hamptons saying that he was a Rockefeller, and another played the country clubs in Sarasota, Florida, where I live. One reason these two wheeler-dealers got away with so much money is that people were afraid to question their authenticity. Don't make the same mistake. If you smell a rat, bait the person and let him or her get caught in lies on the golf course. Don't feel any sense of guilt. You are just using an intelligent strategy to protect yourself.

Arranging the Game

When arranging a game of golf, it's important not to hide behind e-mail or a faxed transmission. Communicate via telephone because you can read the person so much better when actually talking to him or her. Start the ball rolling by saying something like, "Our mutual friend Brian said I should call you for a game of golf." Alternatively, arrange to meet with the person and invite him or her for a drink and/or dinner. Whatever route you choose, exhibit respect by giving the man or woman you're inviting at least a week's notice, particularly if you don't know the person all that well.

As you wait for an answer to your invitation, lie low and listen carefully to how the person responds ...

If the person makes one excuse after the other, you probably should give up on him or her. Frankly, he or she is disinterested. Test this hunch by asking the person out for a drink. Another "no" means that you're dead.

If the person answers "yes," but only after you nudged him or her into playing—and a long pause—this is not a good sign.

If there is a short pause followed by a "yes," this a good sign.

Once you break the ice and the game is arranged, don't be afraid to ask a couple of basic questions relating to life and golf issues. "So, what's your handicap?" or "Would your wife like to join us?" are good examples. At this point, you are trying to simply get a feel for the other person, as well as letting him or her know what you are like. Also, drop hints regarding your ulterior motives such as "I thought this would be a great chance for us to get to know each other better," or "I have a couple of business ideas I'd like to run by you." Listen to his or her reaction to get a further read on where you stand. Additionally, take notes on what you learn from the conversation about the other person's golf game, personality, and life experience. For example, if you hear the person stutter about his or her handicap and say that he or she hasn't played for a while, you could be dealing with a fairly good golfer who's merely being modest.

Really good players, unless they are jerks, will be very low key. Typically, poor players come right out and say they are hackers. I like this type of honest response. The "I play okay" answer is a signal that tells you to brush up on your game. This is probably someone who loves golf and who will most likely give you a good match.

What I think you will find amusing is to compare the notes you made or any predictions about how the person will act and play to how he or she actually does perform on the course.

Two to three days before your scheduled golf game, make the obligatory "Just-want-to-make-sure-we're-still-on" phone call.

Be straightforward in your approach, and a lot more direct than you were when arranging the game. Be sure to confirm the time of the game and suggest that the person arrive about one hour before the scheduled tee-off time. Give the person good directions to the club, and even offer to fax a map and supply the country club's telephone number so that he or she has no excuse for getting lost and arriving late. And don't forget to inform the person about your club's dress code, particularly regarding rules that require players to wear spike-less shoes and Bermuda-length shorts.

I once belonged to a well-established country club in Bronxville, New York. I invited one of the editors of *GOLF Magazine* to play, and he showed up with shorts of borderline length, a couple of inches higher than the knee instead of touching the kneecap. Johnny, the starter at the time, came out with a tape measure. The outcome was this: "Mr. Andrisani, you can go into the pro shop and purchase another pair of shorts for your guest." I did just that, and because I had warned my guest, it was he, not I, who was embarrassed and on the defensive right from the start.

11

Getting Ready

The old Army saying "Proper planning prevents piss-poor performance" should be applied the evening before a golf game. The more organized you are, the better, because getting your ducks in a row alleviates anxiety and induces a sense of confidence. Moreover, preparing like a soldier going to battle helps you stay on the offensive, in control, and ready to gain new information on the course.

Just as you will get a first impression from the person you're playing with, he or she will get a first impression of you. It says a lot if your new friend or business associate shows up late, arrives with an incomplete set of clubs, or dresses inappropriately. However, you can take measures to ensure that you are in a strong position to make the most of the all-important first impression.

Set the Alarm

Set your alarm or even two clocks, allowing yourself extra time to get your act together on the morning of your planned game.

If your guest is late, he or she shows signs of irresponsibility or is not as interested as you think about making a connection. This I find to be particularly true if the guest failed to call the club to say he or she had a problem.

Count and Clean Your Clubs

You are allowed to carry 14 clubs. Because you are trying to make a good impression on your guest, be sure not to leave home with a bag stuffed with extra clubs or a set missing a vital club such as the driver or putter.

Also, make sure that your clubs are clean. Dirty clubs also cause you to lose points.

The player who shows up with more clubs than the rule allows in his or her bag is likely insecure and maybe even deceptive. The player with dirty clubs is disorganized, so don't expect the person to put his or her toothpaste tube back in the cup or keep a neat office. The player who shows up missing a club tends to be very bright but not a very dedicated athlete. Chances are that the person will be a good listener because he or she cares about his or her business and personal life more than about a game of golf.

Organize Your Wardrobe

Lay out your clothes the night before and make sure that your shoes are shined. That way in the morning, you won't feel rushed and will be able to relax and gather your thoughts.

I have found that adhering to a conservative dress code is a safe countermeasure to take, particularly if you are invited to a private club.

When entertaining a guest at your own club, you can be a little more colorful. However, avoid being flashy at all costs.

If your guest arrives at the club in extreme dress, he or she is either very secure or very insecure. Put him or her to the test by kidding him or her about his or her clothes. If he or she just smiles, you know he or she is confident. If he or she doesn't, and instead respond defensively—or angrily—tell him or her that you were only joking. However, take note of his or her sensitivity and insecurity.

Map Out Your Objectives—Mentally

Spend a half hour the evening before a golf game devising a plan so that you can be on the offense and raise your level of confidence. Simply determine exactly what you want to achieve and think of ways to accomplish your goals.

In 1988, six years after I joined *GOLF Magazine* as instruction editor, I was invited to play golf at Westchester Country Club by an ABC Sports executive. I did not know him or his name because I had been out of the country for five years working as a golf editor in London. Therefore, I should have done some last-minute homework during the days between his call and our game of golf. I say this because, when arriving at the course to play, I was unprepared for the questions he asked about my future goals.

Only later did I realize that had I done my homework and conceived a plan of attack, I might have landed a job as a golf analyst for ABC television.

When I looked back and analyzed why I fell asleep at the wheel, I realized that I had settled in successfully at *GOLF Magazine*. Consequently, I did not look at new horizons. I should have, for I would have loved to do television work. The lesson is this: Be prepared for the unexpected. Keep your eyes open for new opportunities and take advantage of openings that can change your life.

A few years later, when in a similar situation, I took the bull by the horns, as they say, when I invited Butch Harmon, Tiger Woods's coach, to Lake Nona Golf Club, a prestigious club in Orlando, Florida.

I had never met Butch, but I determined the evening before our game that my business objective was to get him to say "yes" to an idea I had for a golf instruction book by him and me. The best way to accomplish this goal, I figured, was to plant seeds along the way. I would be sure to mention books I had already written with superstar tour pros and top teachers. I needed to show him that I had a good knowledge of the swing and the elements of shot-making.

So, during our cart ride between shots, I talked enthusiastically about my career, the game of golf, and the benefits of publishing a book.

After the round, at the 19th hole, I told Butch how I thought the book should be laid out, including the importance of including the lessons he learned from his father, Claude Harmon, as well as the legendary Ben Hogan; I knew through doing research that Butch had played with him when he was a young boy.

Butch agreed to work with me on the book we called *The Four Cornerstones of Winning Golf*. Later, we did a second book: *Playing Lessons with Butch Harmon*. My read on Butch was right, and my strategies worked—to the benefit of us both.

Taking First Impressions

When showing up as a guest or when hosting a guest, first impressions are very important. Trust me; you can tell a lot about people just from analyzing their equipment, studying their body language, and listening to how they talk about the game.

Money Talks Analysis

Nothing is worse than being invited to play as a guest and finding out that you have to pay your own way. This can happen at a public course or a private club. Either way, it's embarrassing. Get one thing straight: When you invite someone to play golf, you pay for the day because it usually will "wash" in the end. Chances are, the person will give you a return invitation to his or her club and take care of everything, so don't quibble over the dollar issue and get off to a poor start. Avoid those who do quibble over money because they never see down the road; your business will never grow because they play things safe and tend to shy away from even sensible risks.

In any case, should your host tell you what you owe or make an issue out of money, just keep your cool and make a mental note of this red flag. Sure it's rude, but things could turn around. I've had this happen, and later on the person in question picked up a big drink tab at the 19th hole and paid for a *very* expensive dinner afterward. Admittedly, that's rare. Usually, once a cheapskate, always a cheapskate.

Equipment Analysis

This list should help you gain insights into the person's personality and true golf talent when examining a guest's clubs.

Plastic tube compartments in the guest's golf bag, red plastic slip-on covers over his or her irons, a multicolored street umbrella with a curved handle stuck inside the bag, and a hand towel hanging from a clip attached to the side of the bag are all bad signs. Savvy golfers cringe when they see such gear. Don't expect this person to play well or to buy you lunch. As final confirmation that your guest has no game, look for old golf balls, dirty tees, and a worn-out half-glove probably handed down through the family. The irony is, I read this type of person as fair, organized, and genuine.

A somewhat aged calfskin or kangaroo leather golf bag, knitted headcovers, a mix of new clubs and classic 20-year-old wedges, new white balls, new tees, a golf umbrella (with a straight handle), and leather glove tell you that your guest is a low-handicap player with a lot of experience. At the very least, this person has been playing for a long time and loves the game. Be careful when betting this person. This type of person is often very confident when dealing with real-life issues and aggressive in the workplace.

Players carrying brand-new clubs and accessories can either be hackers or good players. Here's the trick, though, in knowing how to make a distinction. The bad player's clubs will be arranged sloppily with the covers off the metal woods, and he or she will usually not be carrying an umbrella. The good player's clubs will be in good order with the driver, fairway metal woods, long irons, short irons, and wedges neatly arranged in separate compartments. The putter will either be next to the driver or in the same compartment as the wedges. The good player will also be equipped with a good golf umbrella—most likely one featuring a logo of a famous private golf club or top golf-club manufacturing company.

Clothing Analysis

The guy who wears a white golf shirt and baggy khaki pants or shorts is trying to tell you he's conservative—that he prefers to tread lightly in both personal and business matters, and might even go to church on Sundays. If you want to impress this type of person, mind your manners, make sure that you look neat, and approach any business with great care. Furthermore, back up your statements or predictions with financial facts.

I'm always leery of the guy who arrives at the club with lizard-skin shoes, designer shirts and pants, and a hat from a prestigious private club such as Augusta National. This is usually the type of person who drives a 500 S Mercedes or Bentley, wears a gold Rolex watch, and sooner or later will ask you to make some kind of investment. Typically, this type moves the ball in the rough and rakes three-foot putts away, assuming that you consider the putt "good." My read is this: Avoid getting involved in business with this type of person because he cannot usually be trusted.

When you spot the prestigious club logo, ask the person if he's ever played the prestigious course. If he answers "yes" and goes on and on, you're going to have to work hard to make an impression. This person has mingled with the best, and you might find it difficult to enter his circle. If your objective is business, you will have to prove that you know something he doesn't know about making money.

If your playing partner says he bought the hat while watching the Masters at the Augusta National Golf Club, you have a good chance of developing a relationship. That's because getting tickets to Augusta is far easier than being able to play the course—as a member or a guest!

If someone gave him the hat, you're going to be just fine.

If a woman shows up in a tight top, short shorts, or a miniskirt or a man shows up in sneakers, porkpie hat, and dressed sloppily, chances are you're in for a long day.

Body Talk Analysis

Good players usually walk slowly and don't talk much, giving you the impression that they are thinking about the game they are about to play, and are even planning out shots in their head beforehand.

Typically, less talented, less confident golfers will move and talk more quickly, indicating nervousness.

Another way to analyze someone and determine whether he or she is merely a casual golfer or a serious player is to look at his or her hands before play begins (and before a glove is put on one of the person's hands). Good players who practice hard, or play often, have calluses at the base of their left hand's second and third fingers and at the top of their left third finger and right second finger. Casual golfers who play and practice infrequently have soft, callus-free hands.

Golf Lingo Analysis

"I went golfing yesterday," "I hit par," and "I shot bogie on the third hole" are dead giveaways that the person you are with is a certified inexperienced hacker. If you don't know the game, don't try to use golf slang. When in doubt, speak plain English. You'll pick up the terms quickly enough and won't make the embarrassing misstep of misusing jargon.

"I made a good pass at the ball," "I hit a soft fade and stiffed it at number five," "I busted it off six tee," "I made birdie on twelve," and "I made a great up and down on eighteen for par" are expressions common to fine players. Look out!

Being a Good Host

It's important to make your guest feel at home at your club. But it is even more important to take note of his or her reactions to the surroundings since they can be very telling.

Before the round, make a point of showing your guest around the clubhouse facility. Enlighten him or her on the club's history as you move from room to room. Watch how the person behaves, honing in on his or her reactions.

Some club players are very polite and will merely nod when you show them around your club. They might dress casually smart, play a gentlemanly game, have a couple of stiff cocktails at the 19th hole, never look at their watch, converse intelligently, and quietly take care of the staff. You don't even know if they have left a tip.

Some golfers won't handle themselves as well and might seem more unsophisticated. Look out for guests who criticize anything that's not new, such as the old lockers at many established clubs, are very demanding, loud, and rude to the help. Frankly, I dread playing with these types because they are usually so full of themselves.

Power Breakfast/Power Lunch

If your schedule allows, it's always a good idea to invite a guest to a pregame breakfast or lunch because this is a good way to get to know the person and break the ice regarding your intentions.

Breakfast meetings are good because guests tend to talk more about their family who they just left at home.

At pregame lunch meetings during the week, guests tend to talk more about business because often they left their office or took the day off from work to play.

If it's a social guest or a romantic interest, make a point of setting up two consecutive golf games and lunches: one at a public course and the second at a private club. If your guest is just as comfortable grabbing a hot dog and soda in a busy public clubhouse facility as he or she is being served a gourmet lunch on a tablecloth at a private club, he or she is a good sport. If he or she snubs the quick-bite routine and insists on the private club-scene setting, he or she is telling you that he or she likes the "good life." This is not necessarily a bad thing, provided that you're ready and able to wine and dine this person at your club and top-class restaurants.

Whether you're having breakfast or lunch, pay attention to the person's table manners. Notice how your guest interacts with waiters and waitresses, whether he or she orders the most expensive or the cheapest meal on the menu, and whether he or she bothers to ask if it's okay to smoke (or simply lights up).

Cart or Caddy

In Part 2 of this book, I'll talk about golf-cart tactics. This should be a hint that, when entertaining a guest whom I want to get to know, I prefer to take a cart. That's because I spend so much time during a four-to-five-hour round riding that, inevitably, I have many short break interchanges with my playing partner.

Only if you're playing a first-class country club with scenic views should you go the other way and talk your guest into a caddy, knowing that he or she will enjoy it more. Besides, these courses are not crowded, so during what feels like a walk in the park, you can really immerse yourselves in conversation during play and get a good "read."

A good idea whenever you play is to tell your guest that sometimes you prefer to ride, whereas other times you prefer to walk. Next, ask the person if he or she prefers a cart or caddy. If the guest says, "I'll do what you want to do," this is a sign of a nice, but weak, person. If the person answers firmly, "I prefer a cart wherever I'm playing," that's a signal that he or she feels quite comfortable conversing. If the person says, "I prefer a caddy," it could be a sign that he or she is evasive, self-centered, downright snobby, or merely in love with exercise.

Gift Giving and Receiving

Very simple rules apply here: Buying the guest a hat or a sleeve of golf balls, both inclusive of your club's logo, can help your cause. After all, most of us like to receive gifts. The key is to see whether the person to whom you give the gift shows appreciation or appears spoiled and self-centered.

Going overboard is a mistake. People tend not to trust a big gift giver. Ironically, I have found that sometimes the person who showers another with gifts has a good heart and is also very insecure. You can use this weakness to your advantage. By thanking the person and making him or her feel like a hero, he or she is going to be more open to hearing about a business proposition.

Meet Mr. Jones and Ms. Smith

Make a point of introducing your guest to other people in the same line or a related line of work, then just sit back and observe how your guest acts. Is he or she confident, shy, to the point, aloof, good at networking, or for real? Watching the person will give you hints on what's important to him or her and will help you instantly devise countermeasures before you tee off.

For example, if all the person talks about is money, forget the soft sell and get right to the point about how you can help his or her business grow.

Interpreting the Practice Tee

The better a guest plays, the better his or her mood. Therefore, the more headway you're likely to make on the course and after the round, regarding business, friendship, or romance. For this reason, give the guest the best chance of playing his or her best golf by setting the guest up on the practice tee with a bucket of balls, taking an interest in his or her swing, and listening closely to what he or she says between shots.

Reactions to Swing Tips

In your quest to help your guest get his or her game on track, analyze his or her swing and see if you can offer a simple cure for a fault or a simple tip to help him or her hit the ball more powerfully and accurately. If the person tests out the tip and complains because it does not work instant magic, look out. This type always makes excuses and is going to be a crybaby when things don't go his or her way. In such cases, consider the countermeasure of bringing in the local pro. Ideally, you should look for the person who appreciates your help even if the tips you offer don't work. In this case, just say to the person, "Let's just go out, have fun, and get some fresh air—we don't even have to keep score."

Between-Shot Interaction

When the guest's swing is in pretty good shape, start talking to the person between shots. I have found that during preround practice, the guest opens up simply because he or she can look down at the ball and doesn't always have to be making eye contact while talking. You'd be surprised how much you can learn about the person. If the guest stops hitting balls and begins talking to you eye-to-eye, you've got a winner—a strong person.

A bad sign is witnessing the person continuing to hit balls at rapid fire and rarely looking up. Sure, one could argue that the person is just shy. This is not true, however, if he or she makes money in daily life by dealing with clients and attending meetings. This person is avoiding confrontation probably because he or she has something to hide.

Handicapping

The elements of honesty, deceit, ego, winning at all costs, fairness, competitive spirit, and being a good sport all come into play when discussing one's handicap.

Can Your Guest Take a Good Tease?

Whatever the player's handicap, tease him or her about it and then take note of the reaction to get a read on the person.

Start off with something like, "No way. I saw you hit balls; you're closer to a two than a ten handicap."

If his or her response is, "Hey, I turn in all my scores no matter where I play, and ten is my real handicap," chances are the person plays a better game than his or her handicap indicates. I've run into these types of people, and I usually don't get along with them. You can tell that those people are untrustworthy if they agree to play for a higher-than-normal bet.

If the person's response is, "Get out of here," and then he or she laughs, the person is honest and possesses a sense of humor. I like this type because I know I am going to get straight answers.

If the guest responds by chuckling, the person probably plays to his or her handicap most of the time, but knows in his or her heart that on a good day he or she can play well below it. These folks are usually such good eggs that you find yourself rooting for them to play well.

Most guests forget that someone with a good eye can tell what a person's handicap is from watching the player's stance, swing, and shot-making skills on the practice tee and putting green. If you have been playing golf for at least five years, you'll be able to guess if your guest is not to be trusted or has a thirst to win at all costs before he or she tees off. And if not, by the end of the front nine you will.

Bad sign: After shooting a great nine hole score, the person says, "That's the best I've played in a year," or "I don't understand it; I haven't played for so long." These comments signal a conniver.

Good sign: The person who plays well says, "Hey, I played over my head; I'll adjust my handicap on the back nine." This comment signals an even-handed person.

Good Bet or Bad Bet?

The considerate thing to do when playing a business round is to ask the other person if he or she would like to wager a small bet on the game. Rarely will you meet someone who will say "no" to a $2 Nassau. (That's a bet of $2 for the front nine, $2 for the back nine, and $2 for the 18-hole match.) Those who say "no" are either cheap and afraid to lose six bucks, or they are using a smart strategy that you should be aware of. If based on what you see on the practice tee and the person's handicap, you realize you are likely to slaughter your opponent, it's sometimes smarter not to mention betting, politely say "no" to a bet, or make sure that the bet is small. Alternatively, if you don't want to look like a wimp, say "yes," knowing that you will beat the person for the money, but then make amends by picking up the more expensive drink tab at the 19th hole.

You can take this philosophy to another level. I played with a guy who told me that every time he played with his neighbor he would lose on purpose, knowing the guy would buy drinks until the cows came home after the game. Watch out for this type.

Watch out, too, for the person who says "yes" to a bet, but wants to double or triple the stakes you suggest. This type is likely to try to include automatic presses (secondary extra bets) when a person is two down to one's opponent, and play $5 junk ($5 for birdies, $5 for sandies, $5 for greenies, $5 for barkies). A birdie is a score of one under par. You earn a sandie when you land in a sand bunker, hit the ball out onto the green, and then score par. You win the greenie bet if you hit the ball closer to the hole on a par-three hole than your opponent does. You win money for a barkie if your tee shot hits the bark of a tree and you end up scoring par on the hole.

Dealing with Downtime Prior to Teeing Off

If tee times are running late, don't just stand next to the person making small talk. Take the time to get to know him or her better by seeing how he or she reacts to outrageous suggestions and golf jokes.

For example, tell your playing partner that you like to play fast, so you prefer playing "Gorilla Rules." This means that you can move the ball anywhere on the course in order to give yourself a good lie. And you never, ever, take more than two putts on a hole in order to give yourself a good lie.

They might respond by saying, "No, I want to keep an honest score, and besides, I play quickly anyway." You want to watch if this person really does play according to the rules set down by the United States Golf Association. If he or she chooses to play by the rules and then cheats, write the person off.

If the person says "yes" to playing "Gorilla Rules," I know he or she is just out for a day's fun, and I know he or she is ready to get to know me and talk business. Of course, understand that I would never suggest this way of playing if competing in a tournament.

Another way I test a person is by telling a golf joke I know he or she has heard a thousand times. I want the person to tell me that he or she has heard the joke, and not react with a phony laugh. You know you are really playing with a doozie if you hear the person laugh before you finish the punch line.

Another way I test a guest is by asking whether he or she knows any golf jokes. The person who tells a new joke or two is hip to the current golf scene. Because golf jokes change so often, a real player exposed to course play can't escape them. And whether he or she knows it, he or she is relaying to me that he or she plays often. I pay attention to the person's delivery, too, because I like to get a read on how comfortable he or she feels.

The person who continuously tells jokes throughout the round, whether good or bad ones, is insecure and evades real issues at all costs. The jokester who puts up a barrier also often has something to hide.

Remember, your golf partner will "read" you during a round, too. Therefore, realize that even rarely told, good jokes only have a life span of about 90 days. Also, only tell a frequently told bad joke if you want to test your playing partner.

Wrapping Up

Okay, you've now set up a solid base from which to operate. Fairly quickly, you've learned quite a bit about your guest, just by being observant and doing some subtle "testing." Even at this early stage, it's important that you judge the person according to how he or she presents himself or herself. Forget everything you've heard about this playing partner or what you observed about him or her previously. Sometimes, you realize that a person can be such a jerk that you don't believe your eyes. Sometimes, a person can act like an angel, and you don't believe your eyes. Weigh everything, and look for consistently good or bad patterns in his or her behavior. Granted, if your playing partner arrived late and did not call the pro shop to let you know, dressed like a slob, and never looked you or anyone else in the eye, trouble lurks. You can bet that the person just didn't take the day seriously enough and is probably not right for you. Further, he or she has a lot of making up to do before getting back in the "black." Still, the important thing is to stay open-minded and give the person the benefit of the doubt. No matter how negative—or positive— your preround analysis is, carry on. Just as with golf, it's the "score" at the end of the day that counts. Never lose sight of this and remember your goal: to get to know your playing partner better on the course so that ideally you can make the business or social connection you want. That said, let's do some on-course reading and get a step closer to discovering the person's true self. It has a tendency to come out on the links.

During the Golf Game

It's Time to Make Your

"Plays" on the Golf Course

In this part, I tell you how to carry out your assignments during play on the golf course—from the time you tee off till the time you and your playing partner sink your final putts on the 18th hole.

The first tee situation might seem somewhat inconsequential, simply because you have yet to hit the ball. The fact is, you can learn a lot about your golf partner in this setting. Try testing out the mulligan theory—suggesting you and your partner be allowed to redo your first shots—which might trigger a negative reaction and require you to adjust your behavior. This part of the day is your chance to closely observe your opponent and also test him or her. During the round, it's important to bob and weave, to be subtle about your goals initially, and then go on the attack. For example, how your partner handles the suggestion to turn off his or her cell phone can tell you a lot or require you to adjust your behavior.

In the course of a round of golf, which sometimes requires as many as five hours to complete, take advantage of the opportunities that arise. Listen carefully to what the other person says and observe his or her reactions, particularly when sitting next to the person in a powered golf cart. Be sure to get to know the person before you make an aggressive strategic move. Otherwise, you're likely to stick your foot in your mouth.

There are sure to be some hairy moments on the course, requiring you to bite your tongue or go for the jugular. For example, you'd better be prepared to deal with a cheater or braggart. Depending on what's at stake, you might need to reprimand the player or let him or her slide, while of course, making a mental note of any improper behavior.

Because your interests are also at stake, make a good impression by playing according to the rules of golf and adhering to the guidelines governing good course etiquette. Also, do not do anything inappropriate, such as downing too many beers, speeding around the course in the cart, throwing clubs, or cursing every time you hit a bad shot.

Remember, the other person is also watching you and assessing your actions. Don't blow smoke in a nonsmoker's face. Don't make a dumb comment, such as "Not bad," as the other person hits an off-line slice shot. Don't leave clubs behind on the previous hole; you will disrupt the flow of play by having to drive back and retrieve them. Don't frustrate your partner by teaching him or her a complex new swing theory.

The two principle times you should think about making your move are during the cart ride and when stopping at the halfway house for a snack. In either place, you have a captive audience, so be prepared with a list of good questions and responses in case you get cornered. During the ride, avoid being pushy. Be like a boxer who feels out an opponent initially and then depends on the jab to protect himself and score points. When you reach the halfway house, continue verbally jabbing and see how the other person reacts.

Making First Tee Assignments

Get down to business and start scrutinizing your playing partner as soon as you step on to the tee box. Your guest hasn't had time to get acclimated, so capitalize on his or her vulnerability. Here we go! The game is on. It's time to go to work.

Test Out the Mulligan Theory

If you already suspect that your guest is a stickler for the rules and will never agree to the two of you being allowed to hit a mulligan or do-over shot off the first tee, ask him or her anyway. You know the response will be, "No, you know the rules do not permit mulligans." Here is your aggressive tactical measure to show what you are about and see what your guest is made of. You say coolly: "Okay, we'll play serious golf then, the best kind."

If your playing partner should suddenly go quiet, take some extra seconds to get settled over the ball, and hit a shot into the woods, he or she is not as tough as he or she appears and is easily angered or thrown off his or her game. Now really test your partner: Tell him or her to take a mulligan. If he or she does, he or she's a regular "Joe," but so weak that you can easily win him or her over. If he or she says, "No, bad shots are part of the game; I'm okay," he or she's truly tough. Your fall back line is "I was only kidding."

Cellular Phone Warfare

Listening to someone talk on a cellular phone can be very annoying. The golfer who constantly makes calls during a round tends to be a braggart, someone who craves attention. When not playing golf, the same person takes calls during business meetings, trying to look like a big shot. Worse, when he or she gets off the phone, you have to listen to this type of stuff:

> "I'm sorry, that was my wife. We have to fly to
> California Friday for her brother's birthday. But at

least I get to play Cypress Point." (This is one of the most exclusive private clubs in the universe.)

Here's another typical attention getter's remark: "Damn, I ordered my new 500 SL, and it should have been delivered three weeks ago, and now they tell me it's going to take another three days."

If your playing partner can be of help to you in business, you need to get him or her off that cell phone right away. Try this: "I like to shut my phone off during the round, but go ahead and use it if you really need to get urgent calls." Trust me, your partner will never use the phone again. Now you can enjoy the round and talk business, not bull.

Stay on the Offensive by Being Honest

There is something to be said for players who accept logical advice and don't blame you if it doesn't work. They come off looking good. Too many players—especially men—play this "blame game." If you find that your partner is always looking for someone to blame, you're learning something about how he or she would behave in business or personal matters.

Sometimes a playing partner will immediately put you on the defensive on the opening hole. Let me give you an example so that you understand how to deal with this type.

Say that the opening hole on your course is quite narrow and your guest has been slicing on the practice tee. Say, too, that when it is his turn to tee off, he asks, "Can I hit driver here?" Don't say something like, "Yeah, go ahead and let it rip." There's a good chance he will hit a bad shot and come back at

you with "This is no driver hole; I should have hit three-wood."
Now you know that his swing is so bad that he could not have
putted the ball and kept it in the fairway. But you did not think,
and now you have put yourself on the defensive. Stay on the
offensive by making comments like "I'm going to hit three-wood
because the hole is so narrow, but hit a driver if you feel comfortable," or "You don't really need to; it's quite a short par
four, but if you feel good about the way you're hitting it, go
ahead." Believe it or not, often the guy will take the driver out,
no matter how bad he was hitting it previously, slug the ball
into the woods, and make some kind of excuse. One of the clas-
sics is "I swung too fast." That's fine; at least he was unable to
blame you, and you know that you're with someone who is not
able to admit his mistakes.

Handling On-Course Violations

There's nothing worse than playing with a golfer who plays to
your standard, agrees to play by the rules, and then stretches
them, often right in front of your eyes. The same culprits will
do deplorable things in your business or in your relationship.
However, for your own benefit, you sometimes have to be more
lenient with some than others.

Having said that, when playing in a tournament, always call
attention to a rules violation and make certain that the violator
penalizes himself the correct number of strokes.

How to Deal with Rule Breakers

When you're playing with a close friend, it's far easier to say
something like, "Get real, Joe; that's an illegal drop." When a

possible business relationship is at stake, you sometimes have to handle things a little differently. The following are the tactics I suggest using.

In a friendly match, if your playing partner moves the ball in the rough, drops his ball directly adjacent to where the ball landed in the hazard (instead of where it originally crossed the hazard), or tells you that he scored six when you know damn well he took eight strokes on the hole, let him get away with this behavior. I admit to having closed my eyes to this several times in my life if I had something to gain by not infuriating the other person. However, no matter what I stand to gain, I never let someone get away with breaking the rules during a tournament.

The important thing is that *you* play by the rules.

If you get the feeling that the person just doesn't know certain basic rules, explain them to him with this soft touch: "In case you play with someone else in a tournament, I just want to tell you that what you did is against the rules." You will be able to tell if he looks away or opens his eyes in amazement, that he really knew the rule all along but was just testing you. Sometimes, as I said, the person just does not know the correct rule.

If you are quite new to golf, but have a big game planned with a client, at least know some common rules so that you are not perceived as a cheat.

If you hit the ball out of bounds, an area usually marked off by white stakes ...

Wrong procedure: You drop the ball back in play, near the spot where you think the ball crossed the out-of-bounds fence. You then penalize yourself one stroke.

> Right procedure: Return to the spot where you last
> made the swing that hit the ball out of bounds. Then,
> before playing, penalize yourself a shot.

If your ball lands behind a tree, at its base, leaving you no shot
to the green ...

> Wrong procedure: You toss the ball a few yards away
> from where it originally lay and nearer to the hole.

> Right procedure: Drop the ball within two club-lengths
> of the spot where the ball was, and no nearer to the
> hole. Penalize yourself one stroke.

If your ball lands in a sand bunker ...

> Wrong procedure: You address the ball as you would
> in the fairway, letting the bottom, or sole, of the club
> touch the sand.

> Right procedure: You are not allowed to ground the
> club in the bunker. The only time the club's head can
> touch the sand is through the impact area of the
> swing. Penalty: two strokes.

Observing Basic Etiquette

Unless I'm playing competitive golf, I will not berate someone
who violates the laws of etiquette by walking across my putting
line or who uses the classic gamesmanship tactic of opening
the Velcro snap on his golf glove when I'm preparing to play
a shot. However, whether I am playing golf as a guest or I'm
the host, I do not tolerate golfers who show no respect for the
golf course. Golfers who don't repair divots, fail to rake and

smooth out the sand after playing a shot from a bunker, or fail to fix a ball mark in the green are just like the types who throw an ashtray full of cigarette butts on to the road at a red light.

If you think the person might be so inexperienced that he or she doesn't understand what he or she is doing is wrong, start off by lightly reprimanding him or her. Gauge his or her reaction. Does he or she truly not understand the basics of etiquette? If he or she makes it clear that he or she just doesn't care and continue his or her egregious behavior, put the person in his or her place. At the end of the day, hopefully, you will gain the person's respect. At the very least, you'll have an insight into how he or she might treat a business relationship or shared asset.

Utilizing the All-Important Cart Ride

The cart, as I mentioned in Part 1, "Before the Golf Game," is the ideal communication vehicle because you have a captive audience. Walking with caddies does not offer you the same opportunities, particularly if you and your playing partner hit the ball down different sides of the fairway or rough and do not meet again until you both are on the green, where silence is golden.

When you are a guest in a powered golf cart or a host in the driver's seat, realize that this is the opportune time to get to know more about your partner and to make your tactical play regarding business or relationships. It's also the time to be on your best behavior, to observe, analyze, and size up.

Ask Questions and Listen Up

I remember sitting in a bar a few years ago with a friend of mine, when I met a girl who came and sat next to me. I was just making small talk, asking about what she did for a living, where she lived, and how she liked New York City. My friend interjected and began asking her more personal questions about her hobbies, skills, family, marital status, and children.

When she left, I jumped all over my friend, scolding him for being so personal. "You're going to blow it and scare her off," I said firmly. He, who was much older than me, just laughed saying, "You get further by getting right to the heart of the matter. You don't waste time, and you know up front where you stand." He was right.

The same philosophy can apply when riding in a cart with a potential business partner, sales prospect, or new friend. Instead of "small talk," ask your partner direct questions that enable you to know what kind of people you are dealing with and what kinds of "baggage" they are carrying. That way, you can weigh the package to determine if your efforts are going to be worth it and devise strategies accordingly.

When you're asked questions, think before you answer and never lie. Lies will catch up with you down the road.

The following are some examples of questions you should ask, or expect to answer, when discussing business matters:

Is your business privately or publicly owned?

How much has your business grown over the last year?

How do you envision expanding?

Do you see me playing a role in your expansion, and if so, how?

When the person answers, watch his or her eyes and body to determine how genuine he or she is.

It's also best to do more listening than talking. When you listen intelligently, you can see what is behind a comment and get an idea of where the person is coming from.

Don't Depend on Your Memory

Make notes about your playing partners, particularly regarding matters of business.

When playing with a new associate, there's nothing wrong about discreetly writing down a favorite restaurant or club, spouse's and children's names, or golf handicap.

A smart alternative to note taking, and a much safer countermeasure, is to train your memory, and then use the plan included at the end of this book (see the section "Taking a Post-Round Analysis" in Part 3, "After the Golf Game"). With this form, you can "download" everything you can remember after the day's golf.

Change the Subject

Questions are only good to a point. Obviously, you should stop asking them when you sense that the other person is getting nervous or frustrated. What happens when the shoe is on the other foot?

When your playing partner starts asking you a lot of personal questions, especially relating to finances, it's time to change subjects. Changing the subject effectively can help when your partner starts his or her own sales pitch and can keep the conversation going without making you seem evasive.

Another good time to change the subject to boating, skiing, sailing, baseball, theatre, opera—you name it—is when the other person is playing extremely poorly. You'll score points by finding something else the person would rather talk about. In fact, this is the best time to start talking about what you can do for him or her in business, or what you can do together. Just be sure not to sound like you're delivering your own sales pitch. Back your statements up with homework you have done before the game.

Control Your Drinking or Pay the Consequences

These days, with an increasing number of corporate days, golf outings, and lenient club policies, many golfers use golf as an excuse to suck down a few too many beers and have a good day away from home and the office. How much your partner drinks or whether he or she loses control can tell you a lot. Drinking can lower defenses.

Recently, a guy I invited to my club went so far as to go to the clubhouse (at the end of the front nine), order a six-pack of beer, and put it on my tab. Now, I'm not a teetotaler, but I don't normally drink during play. I feel that alcohol acts as a sort of beta-blocker, and I prefer to play with no drink in me and overcome any anxiety that might come as a result of playing a pressure match. Still, I would have gladly bought this guy a beer or two. He just handled the situation in the wrong way, to say the least, and revealed a lot about his faults. It showed me he is self-centered and would not be afraid to step on anyone's toes to get what he wanted.

What I do not tolerate is the golfer who cannot play a lick, but still drinks and drinks. This type is usually an excuse maker. Expect to hear this at the end of the round: "God, if I wouldn't have drunk so much I would have played a hell of a lot better."

I also lose patience with a golfer who shows his or her insecurity by thinking he or she has to down one too many beers just to be one of the gang. Hey, if a golfer can handle the booze, that's fine. But if he or she normally isn't a drinker and becomes so smashed that the day is ruined, you've seen an important part of his or her personality.

If you like to drink, make sure that you stay focused on the game, particularly if you are paired with more serious golfers. Moreover, *know* that you can handle a few beers—or more hard stuff. Golf is a civilized game, so if you can't drink and still behave in a civilized manner, don't drink on the course. Besides, if your guest or host sees your personality change dramatically, your credibility will be damaged.

Big drinkers tend to drive fast, too, and this is very dangerous on wet days. I have seen drunken golfers drive carts into lakes and flip carts over.

Should the person start to get out of control, don't hesitate to say "You've had enough. We're not going to just lose the match, you are going to get us killed driving like that."

If the response is "You're no fun," there's no hope.

If the person says, "You're right; let's talk business," and stops before he or she is over the limit, give him or her a chance to talk. Maybe he or she will tell you that he or she is going through a divorce or some family tragedy. In which case, you can bond by listening sympathetically.

Course Rules and Signs

The golfer who ignores signs that show the limits of where the cart can go and drives near the green or over tees shows strong "loser potential." You can draw the same conclusion about the person who, although told to drive only on the cart paths because of heavy rain the night before, drives on the fairways nevertheless.

Should you decide that this person is still worth getting involved with, you will have to reeducate him or her and break through barriers to get where you want to go. That's because the people who behave in this way tend to be out for themselves and will take any shortcut to win.

Applying Halfway-Point Strategies

Make a pit stop at the halfway house—if not for a hot dog, hamburger, or sandwich, just for a soda and good relaxing conversation.

If weather permits, this is a good time to sit at an outside table and eat and converse freely while feeling the summer breeze blowing across your face, or to watch the colorful fall leaves and realize that life is not all about golf. It's the ideal time, too, to do some further "reading," and bring up business again or the topic of your golf day. You will be sitting across from each other, and both of you will be feeling a lot less tense after getting closer over the first nine holes.

Should the person suggest that you only make a quick stop because play is heavy, agree. However, suggest that you get something light now and have dinner afterward.

If you're the host and the guest suggests stopping and you agree, watch the other person's actions. The usual thing is to stop for a drink and a hot dog. Proper protocol is not to go overboard and order much more than this when the other person is paying. Watch out for those who return to the cart with a few beers, candy bars, and a hot dog—on you. Knowing that the same individuals are the types who want to stay for more than a couple of drinks at the 19th hole, start developing an excuse for making a quick getaway when you are done with the round.

Look for Deceitful Dead Giveaways

It seems that every time I meet someone new at the halfway house because of no pregame lunch or breakfast, I think of the signals to look for, given to me by the movie actor Telly Savalas. (You just never know who you're going to meet through golf and what you can learn.)

I met Telly through John Jones who ran a tournament called *Show-Am Golf*. Telly had taken over the host spot for Bob Hope. Jones's office was in London, where I worked at the time for *Golf Illustrated* magazine. Jones asked me to write the tournament program and to come and meet Telly for lunch.

During lunch, the conversation turned to reading people: I think because Jones mentioned that he was doing some work for the Saudis producing their airline program, and he found them interesting. According to Jones, if you ever hear someone say or do the following things, don't trust the person:

"I mean this sincerely." (Translation: Most insincere guy you could meet.)

"I'm an honest guy." (Translation: Liar!)

"Ask anybody in town, and they'll tell you I never screw anyone." (Translation: Crook.)

He puts his hands in the prayer or steeple position, and then has the hands separate by applying pressure to the tips of the fingers. He lets his hands spring in and out a few times as he speaks to you, appearing to be listening intensely. (Translation: Doesn't hear one word you're saying; he's simply thinking about how he can nail you in business.)

Puts his right forefinger under his top lip and nods over and over, appearing very empathetic about your business concerns. (Translation: He's thinking how he has wasted his time and can't wait to get the round over, get in his car, and leave the country club. In fact, the nods are to himself. He's confirming in his own head that he will stop on the way home and have a couple of martinis to soothe the pain.)

Takes off his glasses to clean the lenses, puts them back on, and then five minutes later does the same thing over again. Next, he puts the glasses back on, and then shortly after, takes them off and starts tapping one of the ends gently against his teeth. (Translation: The guy will do anything he can not to give himself away by offering full, continuous eye contact.)

Many more telling signs reveal a person's true character. You can only learn these as you play the round with a person and watch his actions and reactions. It might be that you notice that the person looks away when you ask him a question. It might be that the person starts twitching his nose when he is uncomfortable. It might be that the person simply laughs when you are looking for a verbal response. Take note, and then make your own translations and conclusions.

Play the Waiting Game

The person who waits for the other person to bring up a possible business connection has the advantage. Should you be on the receiving end, make sure that once he or she speaks, you listen. Your pregame preparation, what you learned about the person over the opening nine holes, and some quick thinking will help you respond intelligently. People love to hear about how you can bring more money to whatever business it is you are talking about; so, without divulging too much free advice, tease him or her with some good information based on real numbers. If the person you're paired up with in the cart is someone with whom you'd like to pursue a personal relationship, be yourself at all costs.

Adjust Your Handicap

Part of attaining success on the course is to exhibit fairness. Yes, you will inevitably run into the person who is out to beat you, and nothing is wrong with good competition, provided that things don't get nasty and that no one loses more money than he or she can afford.

When playing friendly betting games, if you are well up on your opponent after nine holes, tell him or her to take some extra shots on the back nine. Of course, some players will reject this offer, being too proud or feeling that a bet is a bet. That's okay; make the offer anyway because in the end it is bound to help you.

The most difficult type you will have to deal with is the person who loses the front nine and then doubles or triples the bet on the back nine. I usually reject the offer, knowing that when the stakes get too high, it changes the whole tenor of the outing. Accept this type of bet, and you'll see that it is a lose-lose situation. If you win the back nine and a substantial amount of money, the other person will likely be upset. If you lose, you feel you've been had, and you probably will never play with this person again.

Lots of golfers don't believe hustlers exist. Trust me—they do. Some are so bad that, after beating you on the course, they'll buy you a couple of drinks at the bar and then suggest playing poker or gin with the tagline: "Come on, I'll give you a chance to get your money back." Don't buy into this, whatever you do.

Avoiding the Classic Faux Pas

Observing the on-course actions of your playing partners can be extremely helpful in gaining insights into their true character, and thus saves a tremendous amount of time and energy. By the end of the round, you will know the relationships you'll want to cultivate and who you would want to avoid.

I'll dispense with going over the standard rules of etiquette, such as not talking while others are hitting and not moving around while a person is trying to putt. Instead, let's look at some of the mistakes that can have serious consequences when you're playing with someone you're trying to establish a business or personal relationship with.

Watch the Ball

People who fail to watch the other's ball tend to be greedy, self-centered sharks who are usually jealous of successful people and players who play to a higher standard than they do.

When your partner hits an off-line shot, make sure that you mark a point, say, on a distant tree, where the ball entered the woods. This will give you a reasonable chance of finding the ball and pleasing your partner. Nothing is more embarrassing and damaging than to have your playing partner get upset and ask angrily, "Didn't you see where I hit the ball?"

React, Don't Overreact

Any intelligent golfer, no matter what his or her handicap, will be able to tell if you are insincere when you make light of a bad shot he or she hit or when you make a positive comment about one of his or her poor shots. The person will see right through you, so don't bother trying to fake it. Only say "Good shot" if the person actually hits a good shot.

Here is a list of comments that are inappropriate at certain times.

"Not bad." (As the ball slices off to the right.)

"Well, at least you hit it." (As the topped ball rolls only about 100 yards down the fairway.)

"I don't understand it; your swing looked great!" (As the ball duck hooks to the left, near the out-of-bounds fence.)

"Close; you just got under it a little." (As the ball balloons in the air and flies a mere 50 yards before falling freely and plopping down on the fairway.)

"At least you gave it a chance." (As the putted ball rolls 10 feet by the hole.)

"Almost!" (As the ball fades off into the sunset.)

"God, you just killed that wedge." (As the low-flying skull shot flies past the green by 30 yards.)

Temper, Temper

Those who constantly use expletives or throw clubs are using defense mechanisms to save embarrassment. They want you to believe that they are only getting angry because they usually don't hit so many bad shots. This type of person needs to be reminded that, as the sports psychologist Bob Rotella says, "Golf is not a game of perfect." More important, these reactions reveal an immature person who doesn't like to admit making a mistake. When you hear a club buzz by overhead, reprimand the club thrower, letting him or her know that you will not tolerate such behavior.

To Smoke or Not to Smoke

For some strange reason, when it comes to smoking on the golf course, etiquette rules seem to go right out the window. Maybe because they're outdoors, nobody seems to ask permission to smoke.

The irony is that I find some of these men and women who seem to break all the rules to be the type of people who will do anything for you—give you leeway, exhibit extreme patience, work angles within the confines of the law, and remain loyal at all costs.

Don't Let the Idiot Be You

One of the most embarrassing moments for a golfer is to reach the green and have to tell his fellow player that he left his wedge or a couple of chipping clubs on the previous hole or that he left the headcover for his driver on the previous tee.

Don't be absent-minded and you won't have to make that trip in the cart back to the previous hole to retrieve your clubs or have to deal with the embarrassment of looking like a scatterbrain in front of your guest.

You could count your clubs quickly after each hole. As a countermeasure, if you think you can play without the missing clubs, don't say anything. Wait until you finish the round and quietly tell the starter or the pro so that he can send someone out to retrieve them.

Hitting Into People

In golf, a slow-moving group of players in front of you should wave you through. But even if the golfers ahead fail to be polite, never hit into them. You can learn much about your guest based on how he or she handles traffic on the course.

On Long Island at a course where I once taught golf, there was a player who said to his fellow golfers, "I'll just wake them up," and then hit his drive into the slow group ahead. The ball hit the eye of an artist, causing him to eventually lose his sight.

If your guest hits into slow players and gets a kick out of watching them run for cover, it's a sure sign that he is anger-repressive and plainly inconsiderate. If someone should hit into you and your guest, don't be shy: Drive the cart back and politely reprimand them. Should they hit into you a second time, notify the ranger or club pro.

If you and your group are playing slowly, be considerate of those behind you and allow them to play through if necessary. If one of the golfers in your foursome would rather hurry through the round and play poorly instead of letting another group play through, you might find that he or she is afraid to admit he or she might be wrong in other situations or is slow to back down even when wrong.

Leave the Teaching to the Pros

Offering a simple tip to a guest who is struggling with his or her game is okay, as I mentioned earlier. Be cautious, however, about preaching a swing theory of one of America's top teachers to a guest, and be strong enough to put a stop to a host who wants to help you in this way.

People who stand at the pulpit, figuratively speaking (citing the swing theories of Butch Harmon, Tiger's coach, and the like), are those who like hearing themselves talk. They will never be good listeners, which is something you should recall when finishing the round and writing down your analysis. In fact, what you say to them truly goes in one ear and out the other.

Learning About the Scorekeeper

There is an art to keeping score, whether you are the host or are watching someone else pencil in the numbers. Watch what is recorded closely because behind the numbers can be honesty or deceit.

Beware of Cheaters

Let me now reveal some of the classic moves made by scorers and attempt to describe the types of people who make them:

The petty larcenist: This is the person who has one bad hole he can't accept, so he pencils in, say, a six instead of a seven.

The burglar: This person is much more calculating in his or her approach to cheating. The person has two consecutive bad holes and purposely fails to record his scores or yours until a few holes later. At that point he goes back, filling in all missing numbers. The only thing is, in the spots designated for the two holes he played poorly, he now inserts numbers that reflect a lower score; for example, a five instead of a seven on one hole and a four instead of a six on the other. You know what he scored. However, he believes he's smarter than you or anyone else. Worse, you notice that when he went back to fill in his scores, he lowered one of your scores. He figures you won't say anything because he made you look better, too.

The armed robber: This is the person who actually goes back at the end of the round and alters some of his scores, by using an eraser or wetting the card with saliva on his finger, to replace three or four high numbers with lower scores. This is a rare breed, but they do exist.

Dealing with cheaters is not easy, although in tournament play the right thing to do is to say something. If you don't, you are cheating the rest of the competitors. In a friendly game, I would just make sure that you bring to the culprit's attention the fact that one of your scores is not correct. At least then, you can live with yourself. Don't worry; one day his cheating will catch up with him—if not on the course, in life.

When to Rip Up the Card

When you're playing with an important business client who is having a very bad day and he was the one who suggested you play a money game, just say, "Forget the score; let's just have fun." Next, rip the card in half and throw it into one of the waste buckets by the next tee so that he feels good about the evidence disappearing. Guaranteed, you'll have a ball after this, and he will start playing better, making it easier for you to operate at the 19th.

By now, you should have a grasp of your guest's true character and know whether further encounters are in order. In the same way that your cart ride proved invaluable, expect to gain more knowledge about your guest at the 19th hole, over a drink or meal. This setting is where you can make a conversation, blow your chance to succeed, or lock in an already good thing. So be prepared. You might need to call on some strategic moves to pull you through the day and give you hope for another.

After the Golf Game

Post-Round "Reads" at the

19th Hole and a Final

Analysis of Your Playing

Partner

J ust because you complete play doesn't mean your work is over. From the time you finish the round and the flagstick is put back into the hole, it's critical that you do the right thing. Again, remember that your playing partner is reading you. Show good sportsmanship by firmly shaking hands with a partner you enjoyed playing with. Make a quick getaway only if you feel the day has been wasted and there's no point pursuing anything further.

Assuming that the game went smoothly, you must maintain the advantage by doing such things as suggesting a post-round lesson for your playing partner and then a drink or a bite at the 19th hole. The 19th hole setting is your final stage for winning over the other person and gathering any last information you need to read his or her personality.

In this final part of the book, I review strategies for further reading your playing partner at the 19th, the rules for departure, and procedures for the all-important analysis of your golf guest.

Whether your intentions are business or social, the 19th hole is where you want to complete the work at hand. The secrets to success are in staying super alert so that after doing your final analysis of the person you just played with, you can make the right follow-up plays. Should you not be able to finish the job on that day, but you know you have a "live one," take what you learned and apply it the next time you play with the same person.

On many occasions in my life, I've taken advantage of open-door opportunities and used the 19th hole as my office. But there was nothing more important than a time, more than two decades ago, when I was looking to make a transition from golf teacher to golf writer. What I learned over drinks at the 19th hole, I applied the next day when I played once again with the same two people—one of whom would help me change my life.

In 1977, I was vacationing in Bermuda, staying at the Belmont Hotel and Country Club. Upon arriving, I quickly unpacked and then reported to the golf shop of the adjoining course in hope of finding an afternoon game.

"You can join that twosome, father and son from England," said the pro. "Yes, great," I replied, walking to the first tee with my caddy, Birdie.

"I'm Ronald Fox, and this is my son Neal," the man said.

"John Andrisani; pleasure to meet you both," I said, shaking both their hands.

During our round together, I listened more than talked and gave more than took, offering the younger Fox some swing and shot-making tips. The older Fox was sort of into his own game, as well as doing some observing and assessing himself.

Following the round, Fox Sr. invited me to join him and his son for drinks. He made a point of telling me that he was the publisher of *Par Golf* magazine, a monthly publication in London. I nearly fell off my chair and let him know my dream was to write about golf. I did not, however, pursue the issue further. After a few drinks, he made a point of telling me what I owed (even though he had offered to serve as host). Obviously, I could see right then and there that he was frugal. I countered his move by picking up the entire tab myself, giving me the advantage.

That evening, I called the Foxes in their room and invited them to play golf the following day. Fox Sr. said "yes" on behalf of him and his son, and that response was to change my life.

During the second round, I was more aggressive, and I asked Fox Sr. if he had anyone covering the Walker Cup—a biennial match between amateurs from Great Britain and Ireland against a team from America. That year, the matches were being held at the Shinnecock Hills Golf Club on Long Island, New York. I told him that the venue was not far from my residence. He told me that he was sending a writer and a photographer over for a week. Realizing from the drinks episode how money-conscious he was, I suggested that if he gave me two sets of credentials, I could hire a photographer I knew and write the story myself. Besides, I could save him a substantial amount of money and, being an American, give him more insights into the United States' team members.

I had read him right and used the right strategy to get what I wanted—an opportunity to write about golf for a living.

I ended up covering the matches. My story was so well received that it opened the door for more freelance work. My work also took me to England: first to take on a job as the golf writer for the prestigious *Surrey County Magazine,* and later as assistant editor for *Golf Illustrated.*

Golf Illustrated published several of my humorous golf stories, and I was also published in other foreign publications. In England, I played with British star Sandy Lyle, with whom I ended up co-authoring the book *Learning Golf: The Lyle Way.* After much success in England, I was recruited by *GOLF Magazine* and moved back to the place where I was born— New York.

While I was the senior instruction editor and consulting editor for *GOLF Magazine,* I worked in two offices: one on Madison Avenue and the other on Park Avenue. It should not surprise you then that I played regularly with businessmen at private clubs in nearby Westchester County and Connecticut. I also took many business trips for *GOLF,* entertaining clients. Each time I played, I learned more about networking on the course. During my 16-year stint at *GOLF,* I also played with the world's best PGA Tour players who taught me more about "working the room" on the golf course. Furthermore, I got to play with television producers and Hollywood celebrities.

Today, I still play frequently with Wall Street "players" and successful businessmen who continue to teach me new ways to read people and innovative strategies that have proven to work wonders when playing client golf.

If it were not for observing Ronald Fox's actions at the 19th hole and using what I learned to land a freelance job, I still might be teaching golf today and not doing what I love to do most—write about the game.

What follows are the secrets to making friends and influencing people after the round, namely at the 19th hole. The plus factor of the tips presented is that they will enable you to weed out the people who aren't your type and bring into your life those who might benefit you in business or your personal life.

Making Your Post-Round Moves

Making headway via a golf game requires efforts that go beyond golf-course strategies. To continue impressing your playing partner, you must do the right things, starting the moment you complete the round and ending when you bid farewell to your guest.

The Handshake

Whether you felt that the golf-round experience with your playing partner was positive or negative, it's important that you play out your role by shaking hands and saying thank you. Of course, there are different kinds of handshakes. If you had an excellent time, the handshake should be solid. If the day was a lost cause, and there's no future on the horizon for the two of you, let your guest know that through the shake: Let your hand go limp, like a piece of dough. Surprisingly, the other player will feel how disheartened you are and come clean: "We've got to do this again, when I don't have so many things on my mind. I just did not want to overburden you with my problems." This kind of honest comment could open a seemingly closed door, and things could turn around over a drink at the 19th hole.

If you're a man playing with a female partner, you can also use a light peck on the cheek if it's appropriate. Otherwise, use a semi-firm handshake to designate a fairly good day and a light handshake to signal a bad time.

The Quick Getaway

If the other person, male or female, appears cold, removed, disinterested, or disappointed, and you just know that spending any more time with him or her would be a total waste, start making "white lie" excuses that enable you to keep face but get out of Dodge.

Escape line #1: "The round took longer than I thought; I'm sorry, but I've got to run."

Escape line #2: "I wish I could stop for a drink, but it's my night to take care of the kids."

Escape line #3: "I don't know about you, but I'm beat. I'm just gonna run. I'll give you a call."

Once in your car, it can't hurt to try and figure out what went wrong, from both perspectives.

Post-Round Lesson, Anyone?

If the person was solid and someone you'd like to see again, but you can see that he or she wants to leave because of feeling embarrassed by his or her poor play, tell the person to forget the bet if he or she brings it up and then offer to help him or her on the practice tee. Call in the pro, if need be. You can bet that if the person starts hitting the ball better, after just receiving some quick, easy-to-follow tips, he or she will be eating out of your hand at the 19th hole.

Putting Away Clubs and Shoes

If you both decide to visit the 19th hole, get your guest settled first. Suggest that he or she change back into street shoes and get washed up in the locker room. Next, personally drive the guest back to his or her car rather than have one of the club personnel do so. This is not only the best touch, but also you can peek at his or her vehicle to get an idea of how successful the person is. Granted, you can't always judge a person by his or her car; it might have nothing to do with the person's financial status. For example, members of a well-established and famous American family, who have a house on Fisher's Island (near New London, Connecticut) where I used to play golf quite frequently as a guest, drive an old Checker car. Having said this, a Mercedes or Lexus usually is a better sign than a used VW—at least relative to matters of business.

Following Proper 19th Hole Protocol

You're in the home stretch now, but that doesn't mean you should relax or let down your antennae by getting sloshed. Now is the time to be alert and focused so that you can cross the finish line a winner.

Settle Your Bets

Some people who lose a bet offer to settle up as soon as they reach the 19th hole. If they win, their approach is less businesslike. They might rub their hands together and say, "Okay, time to pay up" or "Give me my loot." Then, they might try to soften the blow by laughing. Trust me, however, they are serious about getting paid, so don't even think about beating them out of their dough. People like this exhibit confidence and strength—two qualities that help in both personal and business relationships.

What's more interesting is that some people will get angry if you beat them and then offer to let the wager slide. They will see this as a sign of weakness in you, so make sure you collect.

Other people who lose try to slide out the door without paying. Some will get right down to business and settle up right away, knowing that a bet's a bet.

One type of person you have to look out for is the one who lets you slide on, say, a $10 loss, gambling that you'll pay the beverage bill that will inevitably be much larger.

The other person you must watch out for is the one who beats you for $50, but insists that it's $52. This type will keep going over the scorecard and recalculating the bet and "skins" until things go his or her way. Stand your ground if you know you're right. However, if you've got to keep reviewing the match to be certain of all the side bets made for "junk" like greenies, sandies, birdies, and barkies, just give the person the two dollars and write him or her off.

Who's Buying?

Whether you have won or lost, offer to buy drinks if you are a host at a private club. The same goes for an offer of dinner if you think it is worth your while and you still feel hungry. If dinner is in the cards, tell your guest to order anything on the menu. Then take note: Smart individuals will not order the most expensive item (such as market-priced Maine lobster) because this tactic signals greed or the cheapest entree because this choice makes them look weak.

At most private clubs, cash is not accepted. The member must sign for purchases at the bar, restaurant, and pro shop. At a public course, where everyone can pay cash or use a credit card, losers should wait to see if the winner buys drinks, which he or she should. Should the winner show that he or she is a good egg, make sure that you don't take advantage by ordering numerous drinks. Should you want to have a couple of extra drinks, insist on paying for your share. But whatever you do, don't put yourself in a weak position by getting drunk.

If the winner doesn't buy at least one drink, you've run into a skinflint who you know will be tough in business and likely won't be generous and giving in a personal relationship.

Conversational Strategies

When entertaining a client, warm up the person further by talking about one or two great shots hit by him or her during the round. Even if he or she did not shoot a particularly low score, search your memory for a high point. If the person played so poorly that you can't think of one good shot he or she hit—which can happen—quickly change the subject from golf and then move forward with your other goals.

After you change the subject, make sure that you give yourself time to mix in talk about family, mutual friends, business associates, and sports with pure business conversation.

Proper Tipping Policies

If you're hosting a business client, whether at a private or a public club, you should never let the other person tip anyone. So make sure that you take care of the club's staff members. I learned this years ago from the president of a marketing company that promoted top golf resorts. I once went to reach into my pocket at the end of a day—during which he would not let me spend a dime. I was visiting a new Florida course his firm represented to write an article on it for *GOLF Magazine*. He said, "No, John, I never let a client go in his or her pocket."

This policy should hold true even if the day did not go your way. You invited the person and you took the gamble, so you pay the tips. Besides, this good behavior on your part might pay dividends. Even though things did not work out with your guest, he or she might feel that you are a nice guy and introduce you to someone who can really help you succeed.

Setting the Rules for Departure

After you leave the 19th hole, it's important to continue your good work by doing such things as making sure that your guest knows how to get out of the club and on the right road and by saying goodbye in the right manner.

Homeward Bound

Be certain that your playing partner knows how to leave the club. I have gotten lost at unfamiliar clubs—like the time I drove around in circles trying to find my way out of the famed Winged Foot Golf Club in Mamoroneck, New York, in the fog. After a couple of drinks, my host took off, thinking that I knew my way out. I was too shy to ask for directions, but you shouldn't be.

Say Goodbye

There's an art to saying goodbye, just as there is to meeting a person for the first time. After a good day's golf, let the person know how happy you are about having gotten to know him or her. You'll be able to tell from the person's comments and the way he or she shakes hands if the feeling is mutual.

If the person's a good match, let him or her know you would like to play together again and suggest a date or tell the person you will call him or her. Watch the person's reaction to see how thrilled he or she is about the idea.

Taking a Post-Round Analysis

When the day of golf is over and your playing partner is headed home, it's important to conduct a full analysis and record your observations on paper. Obviously, if you know that there is no future with the person you played with, don't bother doing this. However, if you are not sure whether the person is worth pursuing further, want to confirm your "reads," or would like to have a record for future reference, it is definitely a good idea to reflect and make notes.

Depending on the time, either return to a quiet area of the clubhouse or, if it's late, get out your pad and paper when you arrive home. The important thing is that you do your analytical work while the memory of your golf day is still fresh in your mind. The better the notes, the better they will help you when you need to refer to them at a later date when you are scheduled to meet the same person again—for golf or a nongolf date.

Basic Profile

Don't trust your memory. Stick to detailed profiling and begin by recording the following basic information about the person you played with in your little "black book."

Golf Analysis

Date of Round _____ Course/Club _____

❏ Personal   ❏ Business   ❏ General

Playing partner's name _____

Sex __ Employer (or job, if self-employed) _____

❏ Single   ❏ Married   ❏ Divorced (number of times) _____

Person's birthday and birth sign _____

Names of playing partner's children _____

What does the person like (e.g., favorite sports, hobbies, wines, cigars, restaurants)?
_____
_____

Are the person and/or spouse into the arts? _____
_____
_____

What do the children like? _____
_____
_____

Do all family members play golf? _____
_____
_____

Club affiliations _____
_____
_____

Golf Analysis

Is the person cold- or good-hearted? _____
_____
_____

Is the person more interested in "me" than "we"? _____
_____
_____

Is the person honest or dishonest? _____
_____
_____

Did the person exhibit a good sense of humor? (Recall if he or she liked your good golf
jokes and laughed off bad shots.) _____
_____

Is the person a leader or a follower, good or bad listener? _____
_____
_____

Did the person make average, above-average, or below-average eye contact? _____
_____
_____

Was the person more street-smart than intellectual? _____
_____
_____

Is the person's business sense good, very good, or excellent? _____
_____
_____

Does the person take responsibility for him- or herself, or blame others? _____
_____
_____

Personality Analysis

In conducting your analysis, use the preceding form and ask
yourself the following questions. (Record your answers and
keep your profiles in a single notebook. Additional copies of the
form are at the back of the book.) To answer any question, all
you have to do is recall the person's behavior on the golf course.
Within seconds, you'll get the answers you are looking for.

> Is the person cold- or good-hearted? (Recall how the per-
> son treated the waitress or waiter and other staff.)

> Is the person more interested in "me" than "we"? (Recall
> how frequently the person used the word *I* in his or her
> conversations.)

> Is the person honest or dishonest? (Recall how many
> times the person breached or stretched the rules or lied
> about his or her score.)

> Did the person exhibit a good sense of humor? (Recall if
> they liked your good golf jokes and laughed off bad shots.)

> Is the person a leader or a follower—a good or bad lis-
> tener? (Go back in your mind and determine if the person
> was comfortable mingling and conversing with new peo-
> ple.) Next, recall if the person followed the herd or took
> charge of the room. (Try to remember instances, if any,
> when the person took the time to stop and really hear
> and honestly weigh the opinions of others.)

> Did the person make average, above-average, or below-
> average eye contact? (Recall your face-to-face contact on
> the practice tee, in the cart, and when you ate lunch
> together.)

Was the person more street-smart than intellectual? (Recall how the person reacted when you tried to change the subject from golf to the arts and to good books you have read.)

Is the person's business sense good, very good, or excellent? (Recall his or her ability to cite "real" facts and real numbers, tax benefits, and profit-making ideas.)

Does the person take responsibility for him- or herself, or blame others? (Recall how the person reacted to bad shots and tips you gave him or her that did not work instant magic.)

Follow Up and Work the Angles

One of my closest friends, a New York bond-broker, is a master at winning over potential clients whom he sees as solid business prospects. This guy doesn't wait until the next golf game to continue working the angles. If he likes the person he played with, he buys that person a gift of some kind and surprises him or her with it. I've known him to buy clients box-seat tickets to a New York Yankees game or front-row theatre tickets, arrange for a free dinner at a top New York restaurant, and send a guest's teenage child an autographed photograph of a top pop star. He does whatever it takes to make a good business connection. Sounds pushy, but in the world of business, doing these things can help you beat out a competitor who is trying to win over the same person.

You've made it! Hopefully, through golf, you've scored and can look forward to a bright future that will change your life financially or socially. Hopefully, you also know why you failed and have learned some vital lessons about what makes people tick so that the next time you get together with someone for a round of golf, you will make a positive connection.

Golf Analysis

Date of Round _____ Course/Club _____

❑ Personal   ❑ Business   ❑ General

Playing partner's name _____

Sex __ Employer (or job, if self-employed) _____

❑ Single   ❑ Married   ❑ Divorced (number of times) _____

Person's birthday and birth sign _____

Names of playing partner's children _____

What does the person like (e.g., favorite sports, hobbies, wines, cigars, restaurants)?
_____
_____

Are the person and/or spouse into the arts? _____
_____
_____

What do the children like? _____
_____
_____

Do all family members play golf? _____
_____
_____

Club affiliations _____
_____
_____

Golf Analysis

Is the person cold- or good-hearted? _____

_____

Is the person more interested in "me" than "we"? _____

_____

Is the person honest or dishonest? _____

_____

Did the person exhibit a good sense of humor? (Recall if he or she liked your good golf jokes and laughed off bad shots.) _____

_____

Is the person a leader or a follower, good or bad listener? _____

_____

Did the person make average, above-average, or below-average eye contact? _____

_____

Was the person more street-smart than intellectual? _____

_____

Is the person's business sense good, very good, or excellent? _____

_____

Does the person take responsibility for him- or herself, or blame others? _____

_____

Golf Analysis

Date of Round _____ Course/Club _____

❑ Personal   ❑ Business   ❑ General

Playing partner's name _____

Sex ___ Employer (or job, if self-employed) _____

❑ Single   ❑ Married   ❑ Divorced (number of times) _____

Person's birthday and birth sign _____

Names of playing partner's children _____

What does the person like (e.g., favorite sports, hobbies, wines, cigars, restaurants)?
_____
_____

Are the person and/or spouse into the arts? _____
_____
_____

What do the children like? _____
_____
_____

Do all family members play golf? _____
_____
_____

Club affiliations _____
_____
_____

Golf Analysis

Is the person cold- or good-hearted? _____

_____

Is the person more interested in "me" than "we"? _____

_____

Is the person honest or dishonest? _____

_____

Did the person exhibit a good sense of humor? (Recall if he or she liked your good golf jokes and laughed off bad shots.) _____

_____

Is the person a leader or a follower, good or bad listener? _____

_____

Did the person make average, above-average, or below-average eye contact? _____

_____

Was the person more street-smart than intellectual? _____

_____

Is the person's business sense good, very good, or excellent? _____

_____

Does the person take responsibility for him- or herself, or blame others? _____

_____

Golf Analysis

Date of Round _____ Course/Club _____

❏ Personal   ❏ Business   ❏ General

Playing partner's name _____

Sex ___ Employer (or job, if self-employed) _____

❏ Single   ❏ Married   ❏ Divorced (number of times) _____

Person's birthday and birth sign _____

Names of playing partner's children _____

What does the person like (e.g., favorite sports, hobbies, wines, cigars, restaurants)?

_____

_____

Are the person and/or spouse into the arts? _____

_____

_____

What do the children like? _____

_____

_____

Do all family members play golf? _____

_____

_____

Club affiliations _____

_____

_____

Golf Analysis

Is the person cold- or good-hearted? _____

_____

_____

Is the person more interested in "me" than "we"? _____

_____

_____

Is the person honest or dishonest? _____

_____

_____

Did the person exhibit a good sense of humor? (Recall if he or she liked your good golf
jokes and laughed off bad shots.) _____

_____

_____

Is the person a leader or a follower, good or bad listener? _____

_____

_____

Did the person make average, above-average, or below-average eye contact?_____

_____

_____

Was the person more street-smart than intellectual? _____

_____

_____

Is the person's business sense good, very good, or excellent?_____

_____

_____

Does the person take responsibility for him- or herself, or blame others?_____

_____

_____